HOW TO PRACTICE

SELF INQUIRY

by

BHAGAVAN SRI RAMANA MAHARSHI

Typesetting and title © 2014
The Freedom Religion Press

www.seeseer.com

www.thefreedomreligionpress.com

ISBN: 978-1-937995-79-9

CONTENTS

INTRODUCTION

The quotes in this book are from the book *Talks with Sri Ramana Maharshi.* Some editions of "Talks" have more than seven hundred pages. Only a small amount of the book "Talks" is on the subject of how to practice Self inquiry. That is because most questioners did not ask about how to practice Self inquiry. Placing all of Sri Ramana Maharshi's teachings about how to practice Self inquiry from the book "Talks" into one small book, such as this one, saves the reader whose primary interest is in how to practice Self inquiry from having to go through that huge book "Talks" trying to find Sri Ramana's teachings on that subject. In all of the editions of "Talks" which have been published up to the present date, if you look up Self-inquiry in the index you will find that it barely lists even a small fraction of Sri Ramana's teachings on the subject of Self-inquiry that appear in the book "Talks."

Please pay close attention to the following Ramana Maharshi quote from the *Garland of Guru's Sayings* translated by K. Swaminathan:

"The sage's pure mind
which beholds as a mere witness the whole world
is like a mirror which reflects the foolish thoughts
of those who come before him.
And these thoughts are then mistaken to be his."

That quote from the *Garland of Guru's Sayings* is well worth spending a great deal of time reflecting upon because it completely changes the view of what is or is not a sage's teaching. The assumption by almost everyone has been that if a sage says something, that is a part of his or her teaching. That quote from the *Garland of Guru's Sayings* completely changes that view.

Please pay close attention to the following quote by Sri Ramana Maharshi from the book *Talks with Sri Ramana Maharshi*:

"*Vichara Sagara* is full of logic and technical terms. Can these ponderous volumes serve any real purpose? However, some people read them and seek sages only to see if they can meet their questions. To read them, to discover new doubts and to solve them, is a source of pleasure to them. Knowing it to be a sheer waste, the sages do not encourage such people. Encourage them once and there will be no end. Only the inquiry into the Self can be of use. Those familiar with logic, *Vritti Prabhakara*, *Vichara Sagara* or *Sutra Bhashya*, or similar large works, cannot relish small works like *Truth Revealed* dealing only with the Self and that pointedly too, because they have accumulated *vasanas* (latent tendencies or habits). Only those whose minds are less muddy, or are pure can relish small and purposeful works."

Both of those quotes
by Sri Ramana Maharshi
point towards the importance
of having a small purposeful book
with carefully selected quotes
on the subject of self inquiry
with no commentary
like the book you are now reading.

Numerous times Sri Ramana Maharshi
pointed out the importance of
not getting lost in concepts
in both discussion and reading
as is pointed out in the Step One quotes
in the book *The Seven Steps to Awakening*.

In the book "Talks" Ramana Maharshi
described the practice of Self inquiry
in many different ways.
That is why there are twenty one chapters
in this book.
To each of the chapter titles that follow
you can add the words
"as relates to the practice of Self inquiry."

CHAPTER ONE

FEELING
(1)

1.   Questioner:
Can a line of thought or a series of questions
induce Self hypnotism?
Should it not be reduced to a single point
analyzing the unanalysable, elementary
and vaguely perceived and elusive 'I'?

Maharshi: Yes.
It is really like gazing into vacancy
or a dazzling crystal or light.

Questioner:
Can the mind be fixed to that point? How?

Maharshi:
If the mind is distracted,
ask the question promptly,
"To whom do these distracting thoughts arise?"
That takes you back to the 'I' point promptly.

Questioner:
How long can the mind stay
or be kept in the Heart?

Maharshi:
The period extends by practice.

Questioner:
What happens at the end of the period?

Maharshi:
The mind returns to the present normal state.
Unity in the Heart is replaced
by variety of phenomena perceived.
This is called the outgoing mind.
The Heart-going mind is called the resting mind.

Questioner:
Is all this process merely intellectual
or does it exhibit feeling predominantly?

Maharshi: The latter.

Questioner:
How do all thoughts cease
when the mind is in the Heart?

Maharshi: By force of will, with strong faith
in the truth of the Master's teaching to that effect.

CHAPTER TWO

CONSCIOUSNESS AND AWARENESS
(2 - 27)

2.   Maharshi:
If you know what this waking consciousness is,
you will know the consciousness which witnesses
all the three states.
Such consciousness could be found
by seeking the consciousness as it was
in (deep dreamless) sleep.

Questioner: In that case, I fall asleep.

Maharshi: No harm!

Questioner: It is a blank.

Maharshi:
For whom is the blank? Find out.
You cannot deny yourself at any time.
The Self is ever there and continues in all states.

Questioner: Should I remain as if in sleep
and be watchful at the same time?

Maharshi: Yes. Watchfulness is the waking
state. Therefore the state will not be one of sleep,
but sleepless sleep. If you go the way of your
thoughts you will be carried away by them
and you will find yourself in an endless maze.

Questioner: So, then,
I must go back tracing the source of thoughts.

Maharshi: Quite so;
in that way the thoughts will disappear
and the Self alone will remain.
In fact there is no inside or outside for the Self.
They are also projections of the ego.
The Self is pure and absolute.

Questioner:
It is understood intellectually only.
Is not intellect a help for realization?

Maharshi:
Yes, up to a certain stage. Even so,
realize that the Self transcends the intellect –
the latter must itself vanish to reach the Self.

Questioner:
Does my realization help others?

Maharshi: Yes, certainly.
It is the best help possible.
But there are no others to be helped.
For a realized being sees the Self, just like a
goldsmith estimating the gold in various jewels.
When you identify yourself with the body
then only the forms and shapes are there.
But when you transcend your body
the others disappear
along with your body-consciousness.

Questioner:
Is it so with plants, trees, etc.?

Maharshi:
Do they exist at all apart from the Self? Find it out.
You think that you see them.
The thought is projected out from your Self.
Find out wherefrom it rises.
Thoughts will cease to rise
and the Self alone will remain.

3.   Maharshi:
For whom is inside or outside?
They can be only so long as there are the subject
and object.
For whom are these two again?
They both will resolve into the subject only.
See who is the subject.
The investigation leads you to pure consciousness
beyond the intellect.
Normal self is the mind.
This mind is with limitations.
But pure consciousness is beyond limitations
and reached by investigation as above outlined.

4.   Maharshi:
There is only one consciousness,
which subsists in the waking, dream
and (deep dreamless) sleep states.
In (deep dreamless) sleep there is no 'I'.
The 'I-thought' arises on waking
and then the world appears.

Where was this 'I' in (deep dreamless) sleep?
Was it there or was it not?
It must have been there also,
but not in the way that you feel now.
The present is only the 'I-thought',
whereas the sleeping 'I' is the real 'I'.
It subsists all through. It is consciousness.
If it is known you will see
that it is beyond thoughts.

5.   Questioner:
The Buddhists say that 'I' is unreal,
whereas Paul Brunton in the *Secret Path*
tells us to get over the 'I-thought'
and reach the state of 'I'. Which is true?

        Maharshi: There are supposed to be two 'I's;
the one is lower and unreal, of which all are aware;
and the other, the higher and the real,
which is to be realized.
You are not aware of yourself while asleep,
you are aware in wakefulness; waking, you say that
you were asleep; you did not know it in the
deep sleep state. So then, the idea of diversity
has arisen along with the body-consciousness;
this body-consciousness arose at
some particular moment; it has origin and end.
What originates must be something.
What is that something?
It is the 'I'-consciousness.
Who am I? Whence am I? On finding the source,
you realize the state of Absolute Consciousness.

6.   Maharshi:
Sense-perceptions can only be indirect knowledge,
and not direct knowledge.
Only one's own awareness is direct knowledge,
as is the common experience of one and all.
No aids are needed to know one's own Self,
i.e., to be aware.
The one Infinite Unbroken Whole
becomes aware of itself as 'I'.
This is its original name.
All other names, e.g., OM, are later growths.
Liberation is only to remain aware of the Self.
Though the 'I' is always experienced,
yet one's attention has to be drawn to it.
Only then does knowledge dawn.
Thus the need for the instruction
of the Upanishads and of wise sages.

7.   Maharshi:
The essence of mind is only awareness
or consciousness.
When the ego, however, dominates it,
it functions as the reasoning, thinking
or sensing faculty.
The cosmic mind being not limited by the ego,
has nothing separate from itself
and is therefore only aware.

8.   Maharshi:
He must first discern consciousness from
insentience and be the consciousness only.
Later let him realize that
insentience is not apart from consciousness.
This is discrimination (Viveka).
The initial discrimination must persist to the end.
Its fruit is liberation.

9.   Maharshi: Who sees the blank?

     Questioner: I know that I see it.

     Maharshi:
The consciousness overlooking the blank
is the Self.

10.   Questioner:
How is the 'I-I' consciousness felt?

     Maharshi:
As an unbroken awareness of 'I'.
It is simply consciousness.

     Questioner:
Can we know it when it dawns?

     Maharshi:
Yes, as consciousness.
You are that even now.
There will be no mistaking it when it is pure.

Questioner:
Why do we have such a place as the 'Heart'
for meditation?

Maharshi:
Because you seek consciousness.
Where can you find it?
Can you reach it externally?
You have to find it internally.
Therefore you are directed inward.
Again the 'Heart' is only the seat of consciousness
or the consciousness itself.

11.   Maharshi:
Your Self is intimate to you.
You are aware of the Self.
Seek it and be it.
That will expand as the Infinite.

12.   Questioner:
In my meditation a blank interposes;
I see no figure.

Maharshi: Of course not.

Questioner: What about the blank?

Maharshi:
Who sees the blank?
You must be there.
There is consciousness witnessing the blank.

Questioner:
Does it mean that I must go deeper
and deeper?

Maharshi: Yes.
There is no moment when you are not.

13.   Maharshi:
The Self has no sight or hearing.
It lies beyond all these – *all alone,*
as pure consciousness.

14.   Maharshi: What are you?
You are not the body.
You are pure consciousness.

15.   Questioner:
May I take it that the Self and the non-Self
are like substance and its shadow?

Maharshi:
Substance and its shadow are for the one who sees
only the shadow and mistakes it for the substance
and sees its shadow also.
But there is neither substance nor shadow
for the one who is aware only of the Reality.

16.   Maharshi:
On meditation the relative consciousness
will vanish.
This is not annihilation;
for Absolute Consciousness arises.

17.   Maharshi: The Real Existence
is the only One devoid of objective knowledge.
That is absolute consciousness.
That is the state of happiness,
as admitted by all of us.
That state must be brought about
even in this waking state.

18.   Maharshi:
Before the rise of the 'I-thought'
the concepts are absent.
Therefore you are beyond time and space.
The 'I-thought' is only limited 'I'.
The real 'I' is unlimited, universal,
beyond time and space.
They are absent in sleep.
Just on rising up from sleep,
and before seeing the objective world, there is
a state of awareness which is your pure Self.
That must be known.

19.   Maharshi:
You ask, "But then why is there no happiness?"
What is it that prevents you from
remaining as the spirit which you are in sleep?
You yourself admit that it is the wandering mind.
Find out the mind.
If its 'wandering' stops,
it will be found to be the Self –
your 'I'-consciousness which is spirit eternal.
It is beyond knowledge and ignorance.

20.   Maharshi:

None can deny his own being.
Being is knowledge, i.e., awareness.
That awareness implies absence of ignorance.
Therefore everyone naturally admits
non-existence of ignorance.
And yet why should he suffer?
Because he thinks he is this or that. That is wrong.
"I am" alone is; and not "I am so and so",
or "I am such and such".
When existence is absolute it is right;
when it is particularized it is wrong.
That is the whole truth.
See how each one admits that he is.
Does he look into a mirror to know his being? His
awareness makes him admit his existence or being.
But he confuses it with the body, etc.
Why should he do so?
Is he aware of his body
in his (deep dreamless) sleep?
No; yet he himself does not cease to be
in (deep dreamless) sleep.
He exists there though without a body.
How does he know that he exists
in (deep dreamless) sleep?
Does he require a mirror
to reveal his own being now?
Only be aware,
and your being is clear in your awareness.

21.   Maharshi:
If the light, i.e., the cognizer, or the consciousness
is seen, there will be no object to be seen.
Pure light, i.e., Consciousness,
will alone remain over.

22.   Maharshi: To bring about peace
means to be free from thoughts
and to abide as Pure Consciousness.
If one remains at peace oneself,
there is only peace all about.

23.   Maharshi:
The Truth is that Self is constant
and unintermittent Awareness.
The object of inquiry is to find
the true nature of the Self as Awareness.
Let one practice inquiry
so long as separateness is perceived.
If once realization arises
there is no further need for inquiry.
The question will not arise.
Can awareness ever think of questioning
who is aware?
Awareness remains pure and simple.

24.   Maharshi:
It is certainly something apart from the body
that remains aware.
What is it?

25.   Maharshi:
Everyone is the Self, indeed infinite.
Yet each one mistakes the body for the Self.
To know anything, illumination is necessary.
Such illuminating agency
can only be in the form of light
which is however lighting the physical light
and darkness.
So then that other Light
lies beyond the apparent light and darkness.
It is itself neither light nor darkness
but is said to be Light because It illumines both.
It is also Infinite and remains as Consciousness.
Consciousness is the Self
of which everyone is aware.

26.   Maharshi:
Holding the mind and investigating it
is advised for a beginner.
But what is mind after all?
It is a projection of the Self.
See for whom it appears and from where it rises.
The 'I-thought' will be found to be
the root-cause.
Go deeper, the 'I-thought' disappears
and there is an infinitely expanded
'I-consciousness'.

27.   Maharshi: The Absolute Existence is the Self.
You are also conscious of the Existence.
That Existence is also consciousness.
That is your real nature.

CHAPTER THREE

SEE
(28 – 37)

28.   Maharshi:
See who you are and remain as the Self,
free from birth, going, coming and returning.

Questioner: True.
However often this truth is heard,
still it eludes us and we forget it.

Maharshi: Quite so.
Reminders are often necessary.

29.   Maharshi:
The mind must be cut off, root and branch.
See who the thinker is, who the seeker is.
Abide as the thinker, the seeker.
All thoughts will disappear.

30.   Maharshi:
The changefulness is mere thought.
All thoughts rise after the arising of the 'I-thought'.
See to whom the thoughts arise.
Then you transcend them and they subside.
This is to say, tracing the source of the 'I-thought',
you realize the perfect 'I-I'.
'I' is the name of the Self.

31.   Maharshi:
The real Self is the Infinite 'I-I',
i.e., 'I' is perfection. It is eternal.
It has no origin and no end.
The other 'I' is born and also dies.
It is impermanent.
See to whom are the changing thoughts.
They will be found to arise after the 'I-thought'.
Hold the 'I-thought'. They subside.
Trace back the source of the 'I-thought'.
The Self alone will remain.

32.   Maharshi: See the seer
and everything will be found to be the Self.
Change your outlook. Look within. Find the Self.
Who is the substratum of the subject
and the object?
Find it and all problems are solved.

33.   Maharshi:
People see the world.
The perception implies the existence of a seer
and the seen.
The objects are alien to the seer.
The seer is intimate, being the Self.
They do not however turn their attention
to finding out the obvious seer
but run about analyzing the seen.
The more the mind expands, the farther it goes
and renders Self-Realization more difficult
and complicated. The man must
directly see the seer and realize the Self.

34.　Maharshi:
There is no creation in the state of realization.
When one sees the Self, the world is not seen.
So see the Self
and realize that there has been no creation.

35.　Maharshi:
See yourself first and foremost.

36.　Maharshi:
You are taught the Truth.
Instructions have been given.
See who you are.
That is the whole instruction.

37.　Maharshi:
The only thing that matters is that you see the Self.
This can be done wherever you remain.
The Self must be sought within.
The search must be steadfast.

CHAPTER FOUR

FIND THE SOURCE
(38 – 42)

38. Questioner:
What is the practice?

Maharshi:
Constant search for 'I', the source of the ego.
Find out 'Who am I?'
The pure 'I' is the reality,
the Absolute Existence-Consciousness-Bliss.
When That is forgotten, all miseries crop up;
when That is held fast,
the miseries do not affect the person.

39. Questioner:
I meditate *neti-neti* (not this – not this).

Maharshi:
No – that is not meditation.
Find the source.
You must reach the source without fail.
The false 'I' will disappear
and the real 'I' will be realized.

40.   Maharshi:
The fact is that man considers himself limited
and there arises the trouble.
The idea is wrong.
He can see it for himself.
In (deep dreamless) sleep there was no world,
no ego (no limited self), and no trouble.
Something wakes up from that happy state
and says 'I'.
To that ego the world appears.
Being a speck in the world he wants more
and gets into trouble.
How happy he was before the rising of the ego!
Only the rise of the ego
is the cause of the present trouble.
Let him trace the ego to its source
and he will reach that undifferentiated happy state
which is sleepless sleep.
The Self remains ever the same, here and now.
There is nothing more to be gained.
Because the limitations
have wrongly been assumed
there is the need to transcend them.

41.   Maharshi:
Inquiry of "Who am I?"
means finding the source of 'I'.
When that is found,
that which you seek is accomplished.

42.   Maharshi:

Bliss is not something to be got.
On the other hand you are always Bliss.
This desire is born of the sense of incompleteness.
To whom is this sense of incompleteness?
Inquire.
In deep (dreamless) sleep you were blissful:
Now you are not so.
What has interposed between that Bliss
and this non-bliss?
It is the ego.
Seek its source and find you are Bliss.
There is nothing new to get.
You have, on the other hand
to get rid of your ignorance which makes you think
that you are other than Bliss.
For whom is this ignorance?
It is to the ego.
Trace the source of the ego.
Then the ego is lost and Bliss remains over.
It is eternal.
You are That, here and now.
That is the master key for solving all doubts.
The doubts arise in the mind.
The mind is born of the ego.
The ego rises from the Self.
Search the source of the ego
and the Self is revealed.
That alone remains.

CHAPTER FIVE

THE SEER
(43 – 50)

43.   Questioner:
Who am I?
How is it to be found?

Maharshi:
Ask yourself the question.
The body and its functions are not 'I'.
Going deeper,
the mind and its functions are not 'I'.
The next step takes (one) on to the question
"Wherefrom do these thoughts arise?"
The thoughts are spontaneous, superficial
or analytical.
They operate in intellect.
Then, who is aware of them?
The existence of thoughts,
their clear conception and their operations
become evident to the individual.
The analysis leads to the conclusion that
the individuality of the person is operative
as the perceiver of the existence of thoughts
and of their sequence.
This individuality is the ego, or as people say 'I'.
Intellect is only the sheath of 'I'
and not the 'I' itself.
Inquiring further the questions arise,
"Who is this 'I'? Wherefrom does it come?"

'I' was not aware in (deep dreamless) sleep.
Simultaneously with its rise (deep dreamless) sleep
changes to dream or wakefulness.
But I am not concerned with dream just now.
Who am I now, in the wakeful state?
If I originated from (deep dreamless) sleep,
then 'I' was covered up with ignorance.
Such an ignorant 'I'
cannot be what the scriptures say
or the wise ones affirm.
'I' am beyond even 'Sleep';
'I' must be now and here
and what I was all along in (deep dreamless) sleep
and dreams also,
without the qualities of such states.
'I' must therefore be the unqualified substratum
underlying these three states.
'I' is, in brief, beyond the five sheaths.
Next, the residuum left over
after discarding all that is not-self is the Self,
Sat-Chit-Ananda (Being-Awareness-Bliss).

Questioner:
How is that Self to be known or realized?

Maharshi:
Transcend the present plane of relativity.
A separate being appears to know something
apart from itself.
That is, the subject is aware of the object.
The seer is *drik*; the seen is *drisya*.

There must be a unity underlying these two,
which arises as 'ego'.
This ego is of the nature of *chit* (intelligence);
achit (insentient object) is only negation of *chit*.
Therefore the underlying essence
is akin to the subject and not the object.
Seeking the *drik* (seer),
until all *drisya* (the seen) disappears,
the *drik* (seer) will become subtler and subtler
until the absolute *drik* (seer) alone survives.
This process is called *drisya vilaya*
(the disappearance of the objective world.)

Questioner:
Why should the objects (*drisya*) be eliminated?
Cannot the Truth be realized
even keeping the object as it is?

Maharshi: No.
Elimination of *drisya* (the seen)
means elimination of separate identities
of the subject and object.
The object is unreal.
All *drisya* (the seen) is the object.
Eliminating the unreal, the Reality survives.
When a rope is mistaken for a snake,
it is enough to remove the erroneous perception
of the snake for the truth to be revealed.
Without such elimination the truth will not dawn.

Questioner: When and how
is the disappearance of the objective world
(*drisya vilaya*) to be effected?

Maharshi:
It is complete when the relative subject,
namely the mind, is eliminated.
The mind is the creator of the subject
and the object
and of the dualistic idea.
Therefore, it is
the cause of the wrong notion of limited self
and the misery consequent
on such erroneous idea.

44.   Maharshi:
Visibility and invisibility refer to a seer.
Who is that seer? Solve that first.
Other matters are unimportant.

45.   Maharshi: If the seer be always remembered
it will be all right.

46.   Maharshi:
The Self is more intimate than the objects.
Find the subject, and the objects
will take care of themselves. The objects are seen
by different persons according to their outlook
and these theories are evolved.
But who is the seer, the cognizer of these theories?
It is you. Find your Self.
Then there is an end of these vagaries of the mind.

47.   Maharshi:
When I seek the Self and abide as the Self
there is no world to be seen.
What is the Reality then?
The seer only and certainly not the world.

48.   Maharshi:
The seer alone is real and eternal.

49.   Maharshi:
There must be a seer behind
the waking and dream experiences.
Who is that seer?

50.   Maharshi:
You are the seer.
Remain as the seer only.

CHAPTER SIX

WHO AM I?
(51 – 59)

51.   Maharshi:
Only the quest "Who am I?" is necessary.
What remains all through deep sleep
and waking is the same.
But in waking there is unhappiness
and the effort to remove it.
Asked who wakes up from sleep you say 'I'.
Now you are told to hold fast to this 'I'.
If it is done the eternal Being will reveal Itself.

52.   Maharshi:
He who engages in investigation
starts holding on to himself,
asks 'Who am I?'
and the Self becomes clear to him.

53.   Maharshi:
The feeling "I work" is the hindrance.
Inquire, "Who works?"
Remember, "Who am I?"
The work will not bind you.
It will go on automatically.

54.   Questioner: What should one do
in order to remain free from thoughts
as advised by you?
Is it only the inquiry "Who am I?"

Maharshi:
Only to remain still.
Do it and see.

Questioner:
It is impossible.

Maharshi: Exactly.
For the same reason the inquiry "Who am I?"
is advised.

Questioner:
Raising the question,
no response comes from within.

Maharshi:
What kind of response do you expect?
Are you not there? What more?

Questioner:
Thoughts rise up more and more.

Maharshi:
Then and there raise the same question,
"Who am I?"

55. Questioner:
The world is composed of differences,
from our point of view.
How shall we (be) able to get over these differences
and comprehend the One Essence of all things?

Maharshi:
The differences are the result
of the sense of doership.
The fruits will be destroyed if the root is destroyed.
So relinquish the sense of doership;
the differences will vanish
and the essential reality will reveal itself.
In order to give up the sense of doership
one must seek to find out who the doer is.
Inquire within;
the sense of doership will vanish.
Inquiry is the method.

56.   Maharshi:
Inquire "Who am I?"
Sink deep within and abide as the Self.

57.   Questioner:
Is there no way of escape
from the miseries of the world?

Maharshi:
There is only one way and that consists of
not losing sight of one's Self
under any circumstances.
To inquire "Who am I?" is the only remedy
for all the ills of the world.
It is also perfect bliss.

58.   Maharshi:
All that you need to do is inquire, "Who am I?"

59.   Maharshi:
The best means of realization
is the inquiry "Who am I?"
The present trouble is to the mind
and it must be removed by the mind only.

CHAPTER SEVEN

THE SELF
(60 – 63)

60.   Maharshi:
One-pointedness reveals the Self as being Infinite
and Blissful.

61.   Maharshi:
The Pure Mind, i.e. the mind free from thoughts
is the Self.
The Pure Mind is beyond the impure mind.

62.   Maharshi:
If you know the Self there will be no darkness,
no ignorance and no misery.

63.   Maharshi:
Only be aware of the Self.
Why worry about these shadows?
How do they affect the Self?

CHAPTER EIGHT

THE MIND
(64 – 75)

64.   Questioner:
How shall we discover the nature of the mind
i.e., its ultimate cause,
or the noumenon of which it is a manifestation?

   Maharshi:
Arranging thoughts in the order of value,
the 'I' thought is the all-important thought.
Personality-idea or thought is also the root
or the stem of all other thoughts,
since each idea or thought arises
only as someone's thought
and is not known to exist independently of the ego.
The ego therefore exhibits thought-activity.
The second and the third persons
do not appear except to the first person.
Therefore they arise
only after the first person appears,
so all the three persons
seem to rise and sink together.
Trace, then, the ultimate cause of 'I' or personality.

65.   Maharshi:
The mind is by nature restless.
Begin liberating it from its restlessness;
give it peace; make it free from distractions;
train it to look inward; make this a habit.

This is done by ignoring the external world
and removing the obstacles to peace of mind.

Questioner:
How is restlessness removed from the mind?

Maharshi: External contacts
– contacts with objects other than itself –
make the mind restless.
Loss of interest in non-Self, is the first step.
Then the habits of introspection
and concentration follow.
They are characterized by
control of external senses, internal faculties, etc.
ending in *samadhi* (undistracted mind
consciously absorbed in the Self).

66.   Questioner:
How to control the mind?

Maharshi: What is mind?
Whose is the mind?

Questioner:
The mind always wanders.
I cannot control it.

Maharshi:
It is the nature of the mind to wander.
You are not the mind.
The mind springs up and sinks down.

It is impermanent, transitory,
whereas you are eternal.
There is nothing but the Self.
To inhere in the Self is the thing.
Never mind the mind.
If its source is sought, it will vanish
leaving the Self unaffected.

Questioner:
So one need not seek to control the mind?

Maharshi:
There is no mind to control if you realize the Self.
The mind vanishing, the Self shines forth.

67.   Maharshi:
To think is not your real nature.

68.   Maharshi:
Get hold of the mind.

Questioner: How?

Maharshi:
Mind is intangible.
In fact, it does not exist.
The surest way of control is to seek it.
Then its activities cease.

69.   Maharshi:
It is in the mind that birth and death,
pleasure and pain,
in short the world and ego exist.
If the mind is destroyed all these are destroyed too.
Note that it should be annihilated,
not just made latent.
For the mind is dormant in (deep dreamless) sleep.
It does not know anything.
Still, on waking up, you are as you were before.
There is no end of grief.
But if the mind be destroyed
the grief will have no background
and will disappear along with the mind.

   Questioner:
How to destroy the mind?

   Maharshi:
Seek the mind.
On being sought, it will disappear.

   Questioner:
I do not understand.

   Maharshi:
The mind is only a bundle of thoughts.
The thoughts arise because there is the thinker.
The thinker is the ego. The ego, if sought,
will vanish automatically. The ego and the mind
are the same. The ego is the root-thought
from which all other thoughts arise.

Questioner:
How to seek the mind?

Maharshi: Dive within.
You are now aware
that the mind rises up from within.
So sink within and seek.

Questioner:
I do not understand how it is to be done.

Maharshi:
You are practicing breath-control.
Mechanical breath-control
will not lead one to the goal.
It is only an aid.
While doing it mechanically take care to be alert
and remember the 'I' thought
and seek its source.
Then you will find that where breath sinks,
there 'I' thought arises.
They sink and rise together.
The 'I' thought also will sink along with breath.
Simultaneously, another luminous and infinite 'I-I'
will become manifest,
which will be continuous and unbroken.
That is the goal.

Questioner:
Not clear yet.

Maharshi:
When the attempt is made,
it will of itself take you to the goal.

70.   Questioner:
How to get peace?

Maharshi:
That is the natural state.
The mind obstructs the innate peace.
Our investigation is only in the mind.
Investigate the mind; it will disappear.
There is no entity by name mind.
Because of the emergence of thoughts
we surmise something from which they start.
That we term mind.
When we probe to see what it is,
there is nothing like it.
After it has vanished,
Peace will be found to remain eternal.

Questioner:
What is *buddhi* (intellect)?

Maharshi:
The thinking or discriminating faculty.
These are mere names.
Be it the ego, the mind or the intellect,
it is all the same.

Whose mind? Whose intellect?
The ego's. Is the ego real? No.
We confound the ego and call it intellect or mind.

Questioner:
Emerson says, "Soul answers soul by itself –
not by description or words."

Maharshi: Quite so.
However much you learn,
there will be no bounds to knowledge.
You ignore the doubter but try to solve the doubts.
On the other hand,
hold on to the doubter
and the doubts will disappear.

Questioner:
Then the question resolves itself
to knowing the Self.

Maharshi: Quite so.

Questioner:
How to know the Self?

Maharshi:
See what the Self is.
What you consider to be the Self,
is really either the mind or the intellect
or the 'I-thought'. So hold on to it.
The others will vanish
leaving the Self as the residuum.

71.   Maharshi:
The mind is not you.
You think you are the mind
and therefore ask me how it is checked.
If it is there it can be checked.
But it is not.
Understand this truth by search.
Search for unreality is fruitless.
Therefore seek the reality, i.e., the Self.
That is the way to rule over the mind.
There is only one thing Real!

Questioner: What is the one Real thing?

Maharshi:
That is what is: the others are only appearances.
Diversity is not its nature.
We are reading the printed characters on paper
but ignore the paper which is the background.
Similarly you are taken up by the manifestations
of the mind and let go the background.
Whose fault is it?

72.   Maharshi: Everybody complains
of the restlessness of the mind.
Let the mind be found and then they will know.
True, when a man sits down to meditate
thoughts rush up by dozens.
The mind is only a bundle of thoughts.
The attempt to push through
the barrage of thoughts is unsuccessful.
If one can by any means abide in the Self it is good.

73. Maharshi:
After the mind ceases to exist
and bliss of peace has been realized,
one will find it then as difficult
to bring out a thought,
as he now finds it difficult to keep out all thoughts.

74. Maharshi:
This I-consciousness is present
throughout all the three states.
There is no change in it.
That is alone real.
The three states are false.
They are only for the mind.
It is the mind which obstructs your vision
of your true nature.
Your true nature is that of infinite spirit.
That was the case in your (deep dreamless) sleep.
You note the limitations in the other two states.
What is the difference due to?
There was no mind in (deep dreamless) sleep,
but it exists in the dream and the waking states.
The feeling of limitation is the work of the mind.
What is mind? Find it.
If you search for it, it will vanish by itself.
For it has no real existence.
It is comprised of thoughts.
It disappears with the cessation of thoughts.

Questioner:
Do I remain then?

Maharshi:
What was your experience
in (deep dreamless) sleep?
There were no thoughts, no mind,
and yet you remained then.

75.   Maharshi: 'I' is never new.
It is eternally the same.

Questioner:
Do you mean to say there is no progress?

Maharshi:
Progress is perceived by the outgoing mind.
Everything is still when the mind is introverted
and the Self is sought.

CHAPTER NINE

I – I
(76 – 80)

76.   Questioner:
Thoughts cease suddenly,
then 'I-I' rises up as suddenly and continues.
It is only in the feeling and not in the intellect.
Can it be right?

Maharshi:
It is certainly right.
Thoughts must cease and reason disappear
for 'I-I' to rise up and be felt.
Feeling is the prime factor and not reason.

Questioner:
Moreover it is not in the head
but in the right side of the chest.

Maharshi:
It ought to be so.
Because the Heart is there.

Questioner:
When I see outside it disappears.
What is to be done?

Maharshi:
It must be held tight.

77.   Maharshi:
Only the annihilation of 'I' is Liberation.
But it can be gained
only by keeping the 'I-I' always in view.
So the need for the investigation of the 'I' thought.
If the 'I' is not let go,
no blank can result to the seeker.
Otherwise meditation will end in sleep.
There is only one 'I' all along,
but what arises up from time to time
is the mistaken 'I-thought';
whereas the intuitive 'I'
always remains Self-shining,
i.e., even before it becomes manifest.

78.   Maharshi:
The awareness is the 'I'.
Realize it and that is the truth.

     Questioner:
On inquiry into the origin of thoughts
there is a perception of 'I'.
But it does not satisfy me.

     Maharshi: Quite right.
The perception of 'I' is associated with a form,
maybe the body.
There should be nothing associated
with the pure Self.
The Self is the unassociated pure Reality,
in whose light the body, the ego, etc. shine.

On stilling all thoughts
the pure consciousness remains over.
Just on waking from sleep
and before becoming aware of the world
there is that pure 'I-I'.
Hold to it without sleeping
or without allowing thoughts to possess you.

79.　Questioner:
How to discern the ego from the Perfect 'I-I'?

　　Maharshi:
That which rises and falls is the transient 'I'.
That which has neither origin nor end
is the permanent 'I-I' consciousness.

80.　Maharshi:
'I-I' is the Self; "I am this" or "I am that" is the ego.
Shining is there always.
The ego is transitory.
When the 'I' is kept up as 'I' alone it is the Self;
when it flies at a tangent and says "this"
it is the ego.

CHAPTER TEN

PRACTICE AND EFFORT
(81 – 96)

81.   Questioner:
Is intellectual knowledge enough?

Maharshi:
Unless intellectually known,
how to practice it?
Learn it intellectually first,
then do not stop with that.
Practice it.

82.   Maharshi:
There is a state beyond our efforts
or effortlessness.
Until it is realized effort is necessary.
After tasting such Bliss even once
one will repeatedly try to regain it.
Having once experienced the Bliss of Peace
no one would like to be out of it
or engaged himself otherwise.

83.   Maharshi:
The one then in (deep dreamless) sleep
is also now awake.
There was happiness in (deep dreamless) sleep;
but misery in wakefulness.
There was no 'I' thought in (deep dreamless) sleep;
but it is now, while awake.

The state of happiness and of no 'I' thought
in (deep dreamless) sleep is without effort.
The aim should be to bring about that state
even now.
That requires effort.

84.   Maharshi:
Do you doubt the existence of your own Self?

Questioner:
No. But still,
I want to know how the Self could be realized.
Is there any method leading to it?

Maharshi: Make effort.
Just as water is got by boring a well,
so also you realize the Self by investigation.

85.   Questioner:
But I do not understand.
It is difficult.

Maharshi:
This thought of difficulty is the chief obstacle.
A little practice will make you think differently.

Questioner:
What is the practice?

Maharshi:
To find out the source of 'I'.

86.   Questioner:
Well, can I get realization in this life?

Maharshi:
This has already been answered.
You are always the Self.
Earnest efforts never fail.
Success is bound to result.

87.   Questioner:
Association with the wise
may strengthen the mind.
There must also be practice.
What practice should be made?

Maharshi: Yes.
Practice is necessary too.
Practice means removal of the predispositions.
Practice is not for any fresh gain;
it is to kill the predispositions.

Questioner:
Abhyasa (practice) should give me that power.

Maharshi:
Practice is power.
If thoughts are reduced to a single thought
the mind is said to have grown strong.
When practice remains unshaken
it becomes *sahaja* (natural).

Questioner:
What is such practice?

Maharshi:
Inquiring into the Self. That is all.
Atmanyeva vasam nayet...
(Fix the mind on the Self.)

Questioner:
What is the aim to be kept in view?
Practice requires an aim.

Maharshi:
Atman (Self) is the aim.
What else can there be?
All other aims are for those incapable of
atmalakshya (having the Self for the aim).
They lead you ultimately to
atma-vichara (inquiry into the Self).
One-pointedness is the fruit of all kinds of practice.
One may get it quickly;
another after a long time.
Everything depends on the practice.

88.   Questioner:
The mind becomes peaceful for a short while
and again emerges forth.
What is to be done?

Maharshi: The peace often gained
must be remembered at other times.
That peace is your natural and permanent state.

By continuous practice it will become natural.
That is called the 'current'.
That is your true nature.

89.   Maharshi: It is not external
and therefore need not be sought elsewhere.
It is internal and also eternal.
It is always realized.
But you say you are not aware.
It requires constant attention to itself.
No other effort is necessary.
Your effort is only meant not to allow yourself
to be distracted by other thoughts.

90.   Maharshi:
Why is not that pure 'I' realized now
or even remembered by us?
Because of want of acquaintance (*parichaya*)
with it.
It can be recognized only
if it is consciously attained.
Therefore make the effort and gain consciously.

91.   Maharshi:
The thought-free state is one's primal state
and full of bliss.
Is it not miserable to leave such a state
for the thought-ridden and unhappy one?
If one wants to abide in the thought-free state,
a struggle is inevitable.
One must fight one's way through
before regaining one's original primal state.

If one succeeds in the fight and reaches the goal,
the enemy, namely the thoughts,
will all subside in the Self
and disappear entirely.
The thoughts are the enemy.
They amount to the creation of the Universe.

92.   Questioner:
But the mind slips away from our control.

      Maharshi: Be it so.
Do not think of it.
When you recollect yourself
bring it back and turn it inward.
That is enough.
No one succeeds without effort.
Mind control is not one's birthright.
The successful few owe their success
to their perseverance.

93.   Maharshi:
All efforts are for eliminating
the present obscuration of the Truth.

94.   Maharshi:
Effort is needed so long as there is mind.

95.   Maharshi:
Even a single effort to still at least a single thought
even for a trice goes a long way
to reach the state of quiescence. Effort is required
and it is possible in the waking state only.

96.   Questioner:
Mrs. D. said there were breaks in her awareness
and desired to know how the awareness
might be made continuous.

    Maharshi:
Breaks are due to thoughts.
You cannot be aware of breaks unless you think so.
It is only a thought.
Repeat the old practice,
"To whom do these thoughts arise?"
Keep up the practice until there are no breaks.
Practice alone will bring about
continuity of awareness.

CHAPTER ELEVEN

TO WHOM?
(97 – 102)

97.   Maharshi:
Just get over the false conception
of the 'I' being the body.
Discover to whom the thoughts arise.
If the present 'I'-ness vanishes,
the discovery is complete.
What remains over is the pure Self.
Compare deep (dreamless) sleep and wakefulness.
Diversity and body are found only in the latter.
In the former the Self remains
without the perception of body or of the world.
Happiness reigns there.

98.   Questioner:
Two gentlemen from Ambala
had been here for a few weeks.
Just before taking leave of Sri Bhagavan
one of them asked how he should remove
the spiritual drowsiness of his friends
or of other people in general.

    Maharshi:
Have you removed your own
'spiritual drowsiness?'
The force which is set up
to remove your own 'drowsiness'
will also operate in other centers.

There is the will-power
with which you can act on others.
But it is on a lower plane
and not desirable.
Take care of yourself first.

Questioner:
How to remove my own 'drowsiness'?

Maharshi:
Whose 'drowsiness' is it.
Inquire. Turn within.
Turn all your inquiries towards search for Self.
The force set up within you
will operate on others also.

99.   Maharshi:
For whom is this relativity?
For whom is this imperfection?
The Absolute is not imperfect and cannot ask.
The insentient cannot ask the question.
Between the two something has risen up
which raises these questions
and which feels this doubt.
Who is it?
Is it the one who has now arisen?
Or is it the one who is eternal?

100. Maharshi:
Inquire to whom these questions arise.
Dive deep in the Heart and remain as the Self.

101. Maharshi:
"Why and to whom did this suffering come?"
If you question thus you will find that the 'I'
is separate from the mind and body,
that the Self is the only eternal being,
and that It is eternal bliss.

102. Maharshi:
See for whom this question arises.
Unless the questioner is found,
the questions can never be set at rest.

CHAPTER TWELVE

THE HEART
(103 – 107)

103. Maharshi: To see the objects
the reflected light of the mind is necessary.
To see the Heart
it is enough that the mind is turned towards it.
Then the mind loses itself
and the Heart shines forth.

104. Questioner:
How is the mind to dive into the Heart?

Maharshi:
The mind now sees itself
diversified as the universe.
If the diversity is not manifest
it remains in its own essence,
that is the Heart.
Entering the Heart means
remaining without distractions.
The Heart is the only Reality.
The mind is only a transient phase.
To remain as one's Self is to enter the Heart.

105. Maharshi:
I want you to dive consciously into the Self,
i.e., into the Heart.

106. Questioner:
Should I meditate on the right chest
in order to meditate on the Heart?

Maharshi:
The Heart is not physical.
Meditation should not be on the right or the left.
Meditation should be on the Self.
Everyone knows 'I am'.
Who is the 'I'?
It will be neither within nor without,
neither on the right nor on the left.
'I am' – that is all.

107. Maharshi:
Bliss consists in not forgetting your being.
How can you be otherwise
than what you really are?
It is also the Seat of Love.
Love is Bliss.
Here the Seat is not different from Love.

CHAPTER THIRTEEN

I
(108 – 119)

108. Questioner:
Some men asked the Master questions
which ultimately resolved themselves into one,
that 'I' is not perceptible
however much they might struggle.

    Maharshi:
Who is it that says that 'I' is not perceptible?
Is there an 'I' ignorant,
and an 'I' elusive?
Are there two 'I's in the same person?
Ask yourself these questions.
It is the mind which says that 'I' is not perceptible.
Where is that mind from?
Know the mind.
You will find it a myth.
King Janaka said,
'I have discovered the thief
who had been ruining me so long.
I will now deal with him summarily.
Then I shall be happy.'
Similarly it will be with others.

109. Questioner:
How to realize Self?

Maharshi:
Whose Self? Find out.

Questioner:
Who am I?

Maharshi:
Find it yourself.

Questioner:
I do not know.

Maharshi: Think.
Who is it that says "I do not know?"
What is not known?
In that statement, who is this 'I'?

Questioner:
Somebody in me.

Maharshi:
Who is the somebody?
In whom?

Questioner:
Maybe some power.

Maharshi: Find it.

110. Maharshi:
"I heard the recital," you say.
Who is that I?
Without knowing the 'I' you are using the word.
If its significance be known there will be no doubt.
Find the 'I' first
and you may afterwards speak of other matters.

111. Questioner:
If 'I' am always – here and now,
why do I not feel so?

        Maharshi: That is it.
Who says it is not felt?
Does the real 'I' say it or the false 'I'?
Examine it.
You will find it is the wrong 'I'.
The wrong 'I' is the obstruction.
It has to be removed
in order that the true 'I' may not be hidden.

112. Maharshi:
The 'I' which rises will also subside.
That is the individual 'I'
or the 'I' concept.
That which does not rise will not subside.
It is and will be for ever.
That is the universal 'I',
the perfect 'I',
or realization of the Self.

113. Maharshi:
The body being insentient cannot say 'I'.
The Self being infinite cannot say 'I' either.
Who then says 'I'?

Questioner:
I do not yet understand.
How to find the 'I'?

Maharshi:
Find out where from this 'I' arises.
Then this 'I' will disappear
and the infinite Self will remain.
This 'I' is only the knot between the sentient
and the insentient.
The body is not 'I',
the Self is not 'I'.
Who, then, is the 'I'?
Wherefrom does it arise?

114. Maharshi:
Mind, ego, intellect are all different names
for one single inner organ.
The mind is only the aggregate of thoughts.
Thoughts cannot exist but for the ego.
So all thoughts are pervaded by ego.
See wherefrom the 'I' rises
and the other thoughts will disappear.

Questioner:
What remains over cannot be 'I',
but Pure Consciousness.

Maharshi: Quite so.
You start seeking happiness.
On analysis you find that
misery is caused by thoughts.
They are called mind.
While trying to control the mind you seek the 'I'
and get fixed in Being-Knowledge-Bliss.

115.   Maharshi:
Who is this 'I'?
It cannot be the body nor the mind
as we have seen before.
This 'I' is the one who experiences the waking,
dream and sleep states.

116.   Maharshi:
Who is the 'I'?
Whose is the ignorance!

117.   Maharshi:
The functions of the waking state
are those of the ego
which is synonymous with the 'I'.
Find out who this 'I' is.
On doing so and abiding as 'I',
all these doubts will be cleared up.

118. Questioner:
I want knowledge.

Maharshi:
Who wants knowledge?

Questioner: I want it.

Maharshi: Who is that 'I'?
Find the 'I' and then see later
what further knowledge is required.

119. Maharshi: What is needed is
to fix the attention on the pure 'I'
after the subsidence of all thoughts
and not to lose hold of it.
This has to be described
as an extremely subtle thought;
else it cannot be spoken of at all,
since it is no other than the Real Self.

CHAPTER FOURTEEN

THE EGO
(120 – 135)

120. Maharshi:
The sea is not aware of its wave.
Similarly the Self is not aware of its ego.

121. Maharshi:
Hold yourself and the ego will vanish.
Until then the sage will be saying, "There is."
The ignorant will be asking "Where?"

Questioner:
The crux of the problem lies in "Know Thyself."

Maharshi: Yes. Quite so.

122. Questioner:
I do not know if the Self is different from the ego.

Maharshi:
How were you in your deep (dreamless) sleep?

Questioner:
I do not know.

Maharshi: Who does not know?
Is it not the waking self?
Do you deny your existence
in your deep (dreamless) sleep?

Questioner:
I was and I am;
but I do not know who was
in deep (dreamless) sleep.

Maharshi: Exactly.
The man awake says that he did not know anything
in the state of (deep dreamless) sleep.
Now he sees objects and knows that he is there;
whereas in deep (dreamless) sleep
there were no objects,
no spectator, etc.
The same one who is now speaking
was in deep (dreamless) sleep also.
What is the difference between these two states?
There are objects and play of senses now
which were not in (deep dreamless) sleep.
A new entity, the ego,
has risen up in the meantime,
it plays through the senses,
sees the objects,
confounds itself with the body
and says that the Self is the ego.
In reality, what was in deep (dreamless) sleep
continues to exist now too.
The Self is changeless.
It is the ego that has come between.
That which rises and sets is the ego;
that which remains changeless is the Self.

123. Maharshi:
Take no notice of the ego and its activities,
but see only the light behind.
The ego is the I-thought.
The true 'I' is the Self.

124. Questioner:
How to get rid of fear?

        Maharshi:
What is fear?
It is only a thought.
If there is anything besides the Self
there is reason to fear.
Who sees the second?
First the ego arises and sees objects as external.
If the ego does not rise,
the Self alone exists
and there is no second.
For anything external to oneself
implies the seer within.
Seeking it, there will arise no doubt,
no fear – not only fear,
all other thoughts centered around the ego
will disappear along with it.

        Questioner:
This method seems to be quicker
than the usual one of cultivating qualities
alleged necessary for salvation?

Maharshi: Yes.
All bad qualities center round the ego.
When the ego is gone Realization results by itself.
There are neither good nor bad qualities
in the Self.
The Self is free from qualities.
Qualities pertain to the mind only.

125. Maharshi:
Reality is simply the loss of the ego.
Destroy the ego by seeking its identity.
Because the ego is no entity
it will automatically vanish
and Reality will shine forth by itself.
This is the direct method.
Whereas all other methods are done,
only retaining the ego.
In those paths there arise so many doubts
and the eternal question remains
to be tackled finally.
But in this method
the final question is the only one
and it is raised from the very beginning.

126. Maharshi:
The quest "Who am I?"
is the axe with which to cut off the ego.

127. Maharshi:
Seeking the ego, i.e., its source, ego disappears.
What is left over is the Self.
This method is the direct one.

Questioner:
Then what am I to do?

Maharshi:
To hold on to the Self.

Questioner: How?

Maharshi:
Even now you are the Self.
But you are confounding this consciousness
with the absolute consciousness.
This false identification is due to ignorance.
Ignorance disappears along with the ego.
Killing the ego is the only thing to accomplish.

128. Maharshi:
There was no ego in (deep dreamless) sleep.
The birth of the ego
is called the birth of the person.
There is no other kind of birth.
Whatever is born is bound to die.
Kill the ego:
there is no fear of recurring death
for what is once dead.
The Self remains even after the death of the ego.
That is Bliss – that is Immortality.

Questioner:
How is that to be done?

Maharshi:
See for whom these doubts exist.
Who is the doubter?
Who is the thinker?
That is the ego. Hold it.
The other thoughts will die away.
The ego is left pure;
see from where the ego arises.
That is pure consciousness.

129. Maharshi:
The ego in its purity is experienced
in intervals between two states or two thoughts.
Ego is like a caterpillar which leaves its hold
only after catching another.
Its true nature can be found
when it is out of contact with objects or thoughts.

130. Maharshi:
The mind is a bundle of thoughts.
The thoughts arise because there is the thinker.
The thinker is the ego.
The ego, if sought, will automatically vanish.
The ego and the mind are the same.
The ego is the root-thought
from which all other thoughts arise.

131. Questioner:
What is the ego-self?

   Maharshi:
The ego-self appears and disappears
and is transitory,
whereas the real Self always abides permanent.
Though you are actually the true Self
yet you wrongly identify the real Self
with the ego-self.

132. Maharshi:
The Self is Pure Consciousness.
Yet the man identifies himself with the body
which is itself insentient
and does not say "I am the body" of its own accord.
Someone else says so.
The unlimited Self does not.
Who else is he that says so?
A spurious 'I' arises
between the Pure Consciousness
and the insentient body
and imagines itself limited to the body.
Seek this and it will vanish as a phantom.
That phantom is the ego,
or the mind
or the individuality.

133. Maharshi:
Uncertainties, doubts and fears
are natural to everyone until the Self is realized.
They are inseparable from the ego,
rather they are the ego.

Questioner:
How are they to disappear?

Maharshi:
They are the ego.
If the ego goes they go with it.
The ego is itself unreal.
What is the ego? Inquire.
The body is insentient and cannot say 'I'.
The Self is pure consciousness and non-dual.
It cannot say 'I'.
No one says 'I' in (deep dreamless) sleep.
What is the ego then?
It is something intermediate
between the inert body and the Self.
It has no *locus standi*.
If sought for it vanishes like a ghost.
You see, a man imagines
that there is something by his side in darkness;
it may be some dark object.
If he looks closely the ghost is not to be seen,
but some dark object
which he could identify as a tree or a post, etc.
If he does not look closely
the ghost strikes terror in the person.

All that is required is only to look closely
and the ghost vanishes.
The ghost was never there.
So also with the ego.
It is an intangible link
between the body and Pure Consciousness.
It is not real.
So long as one does not look closely
it continues to give trouble.
But when one looks for it,
it is found not to exist.

134. Maharshi:
If you seek the ego you will find it does not exist.
That is the way to destroy it.

135. Maharshi:
So it is with the ego.
Look for it and it will not be found.
That is the way to get rid of it.

CHAPTER FIFTEEN

THE I THOUGHT
(136 – 146)

136. Maharshi:
All that we need to do is to remove the obstruction.
That which is eternal is not known to be so
because of ignorance.
Ignorance is the obstruction.
Get over the ignorance and all will be well.
The ignorance is identical with the 'I-thought'.
Find its source and it will vanish.
The 'I-thought' is like a spirit,
which, although not palpable,
rises up simultaneously with the body,
flourishes, and disappears with it.
The body-consciousness is the wrong 'I'.
Give up this body-consciousness.
It is done by seeking the source 'I'.
The body does not say 'I am'.
It is you who say, 'I am the body!'
Find out who this 'I' is.
Seeking its source it will vanish.

Questioner:
Then, will there be bliss?

Maharshi:
Bliss is coeval with Being-Consciousness.
All the arguments relating to the eternal Being
of that Bliss apply to Bliss also.
Your nature is Bliss.
Ignorance is now hiding that Bliss.
Remove the ignorance for Bliss to be freed.

137. Maharshi:
Forgetfulness and thought are for 'I-thought' only.
Hold it; it will disappear as a phantom.
What remains over is the real 'I'.
That is the Self.

138. Maharshi:
Wherefrom is the 'I' thought?
Probe into it.
The 'I-thought' will vanish.
The Supreme Self will shine forth of itself.

139. Questioner:
How to search for the mind?

Maharshi:
The mind is only a bundle of thoughts.
The thoughts have their root in the 'I-thought'.
He quoted; "Whoever investigates the origin
of the 'I-thought', for him the ego perishes.
This is the true investigation."

The true 'I' is then found shining by itself.

Questioner:
This 'I-thought' rises from me.
But I do not know the Self.

Maharshi:
All these are only mental concepts.
You are now identifying yourself with a wrong 'I',
which is the 'I-thought'.
This 'I-thought' rises and sinks,
whereas the true significance of 'I' is beyond both.
There cannot be a break in your being.
You, who slept, are also now awake.
There was not unhappiness
in your deep (dreamless) sleep.
Whereas it exists now.
What is it that has happened now
so that this difference is experienced?
There was no 'I-thought'
in your (deep dreamless) sleep,
whereas it is present now.
The true 'I' is not apparent
and the false 'I' is parading itself.
This false 'I'
is the obstacle to your right knowledge.
Find out wherefrom this false 'I' arises.
Then it will disappear.
You will be only what you are –
i.e., absolute Being.

Questioner:
How to do it?
I have not succeeded so far.

Maharshi:
Search for the source of the 'I-thought'.
That is all that one has to do.
The universe exists on account of the 'I-thought'.
If that ends there is an end of misery also.
The false 'I' will end only when its source is sought.

140. Maharshi:
The sense of body is a thought;
the thought is of the mind,
the mind rises after the 'I-thought',
the 'I-thought' is the root thought.
If that is held, the other thoughts will disappear.
There will then be no body, no mind,
not even the ego.

Questioner:
What will remain then?

Maharshi:
The Self in its purity.

141. Maharshi:
Get rid of the 'I-thought'.
So long as 'I' is alive, there is grief.
When 'I' ceases to exist, there is no grief.
Consider the state of (deep dreamless) sleep!

Questioner: Yes.
But when I take to the 'I-thought',
other thoughts arise and disturb me.

Maharshi:
See whose thoughts they are.
They will vanish.
They have their root in the single 'I-thought'.
Hold to it and they will disappear.

142. Maharshi:
Now, what is this 'I-thought'?
Is it the subject or the object,
in the scheme of things?
Inasmuch as it witnesses all other objects
in the waking and dream states,
or at any rate we think that it does so,
it must be considered to be the subject.
On realizing the pure Self, however,
it will be an object only.
Whose is this 'I-thought'?
This investigation forms the *vichara*.

143. Maharshi: Whose is the body?
You were without it
in your deep (dreamless) sleep.
After the 'I-thought' arose, the body arose.
The first birth is that of 'I-thought'.
The body has its birth subsequent to 'I-thought'.
So its birth is secondary.
Get rid of the primary cause
and the secondary one will disappear by itself.

144. Questioner:
How is that 'I-thought' to be checked from rising?

Maharshi:
By Self-quest.

145. Questioner:
How did the wrong identity arise?

Maharshi:
Due to thoughts.
If these thoughts are put an end to,
the real Self should shine forth of itself.

Questioner:
How are these thoughts to be ended?

Maharshi:
Find out their basis.
All of them are strung on the single 'I-thought'.
Quell it; all others are quashed.
Moreover,
there is no use knowing all except the Self.
If the Self is known all others become known.
Hence is Self-realization
the primary and sole duty of man.

Questioner:
How to quell the 'I-thought'?

Maharshi:
If its source is sought it does not arise,
and thus it is quelled.

Questioner:
Where and how to find it?

Maharshi:
It is in fact the consciousness
which enables the individuals to function
in different ways.
Pure Consciousness is the Self.
All that is required to realize the Self
is to "Be Still."

146. Questioner:
Am I to think "Who am I?"

Maharshi:
You have known that the 'I-thought' springs forth.
Hold the 'I-thought' and find its *moola* (source).

CHAPTER SIXTEEN

DISTRACTIONS
(147 – 150)

147. Questioner:
How to prevent the mind from being distracted?

Maharshi:
You see the objects on forgetting your own Self.
If you keep hold of your Self,
you will not see the objective world.

148. Questioner:
Are there any aids to (1) concentration
and (2) casting off distractions?

Maharshi:
Physically the digestive and other organs
are kept free from irritation.
Therefore food is regulated both in quantity
and quality.
Non-irritants are eaten, avoiding chilies,
excess of salt, onions, wine, opium, etc.
Avoid constipation, drowsiness and excitement,
and all foods which induce them.
Mentally take interest in one thing
and fix the mind on it.
Let such interest be all-absorbing
to the exclusion of everything else.
This is dispassion (*vairagya*)
and concentration.

Questioner:
Distractions result from inherited tendencies.
Can they be cast off too?

Maharshi: Yes.
Many have done so. Believe it!
They did so because they believed they could.
Vasanas (predispositions) can be obliterated.
It is done by concentration on that
which is free from *vasanas* (predispositions)
and yet is their core.

Questioner:
How long is the practice to continue?

Maharshi:
Till success is achieved
and until yoga-liberation becomes permanent.
Success begets success.
If one distraction is conquered
the next is conquered and so on,
until all are finally conquered.
The process is like reducing an enemy's fort
by slaying its man-power one by one,
as each issues out.

Questioner:
What is the goal of this process?

Maharshi:
Realizing the Real.

Questioner:
What is the nature of Reality?

Maharshi:
(a) Existence without beginning or end – eternal.
(b) Existence everywhere, endless, infinite.
(c) Existence underlying all forms, all changes,
all forces, all matter and all spirit.
The many change and pass away,
whereas the One always endures.
(d) The one displacing the triads,
i.e., the knower, the knowledge and the known.
The triads are only appearances in time and space,
whereas the Reality lies beyond and behind them.
They are like a mirage over the Reality.
They are the result of delusion.

Questioner:
If 'I' also be an illusion,
who then casts off the illusion?

Maharshi:
The 'I' casts off the illusion of 'I'
and yet remains as 'I'.
Such is the paradox of Self-Realization.
The realized do not see any contradiction in it.

149. Questioner:
Is solitude necessary for *vichara* (inquiry)?

Maharshi:
There is solitude everywhere.
The individual is solitary always.
His business is to find it out within,
and not seek it without.

Questioner:
The work-a-day world is distracting.

Maharshi:
Do not allow yourself to be distracted.
Inquire for whom there is distraction.
It will not afflict you after a little practice.

Questioner:
Even the attempt is impossible.

Maharshi:
Make it and it will be found not so difficult.

Questioner:
But the answer does not come
for the search inward.

Maharshi:
The inquirer is the answer
and no other answer can come.
What comes afresh cannot be true.
What always is, is true.

150. Questioner:
Meditation is with mind
in the *jagrat* (waking) state.
There is mind in dream also.
Why is there no meditation in dream?
Nor is it possible?

Maharshi:
Ask it in the dream.
You are told to meditate now
and find who you are.
Instead of doing it you ask
"Why is there no meditation in dream or in sleep?"
If you find out for whom there is *jagrat* (waking),
it will be clear that dream and sleep
are also for the same one.
You are the witness of *jagrat* (waking),
svapna (dream) and *sushupti* (sleep) –
rather, they pass before you.
Because you are out of meditation now,
these questions arise.
Stick to meditation
and see if these questions arise.

CHAPTER SEVENTEEN

THE WORLD
(151 – 154)

151. Maharshi:
When you see the world
you have lost hold of the Self.
On the contrary,
hold the Self and the world will not appear.

152. Maharshi:
The world cannot be seen either in pure ignorance
as in (deep dreamless) sleep,
or in pure light as in Self-Realization.

153. Maharshi:
Time and space are functions of thoughts.
If thoughts do not arise
there will be no future or the Earth.

154. Maharshi:
Until realization there will be Karma,
i.e., action and reaction;
after realization there will be no Karma, no world.

CHAPTER EIGHTEEN

THOUGHT
(155 – 163)

155. Questioner:
Are good thoughts helpful for Realization?
Are they not authentic *via media*,
a lower rung of the ladder to Realization?

Maharshi:
Yes – this way: They keep off bad thoughts.
They must themselves disappear
before the state of Realization.

Questioner:
But are not creative thoughts
an aspect of Realization
and therefore helpful?

Maharshi:
Helpful only in the way said before.
They must all disappear in the Self.
Thoughts, good or bad,
take you farther and not nearer,
because the Self is more intimate than thoughts.
You are the Self,
whereas thoughts are alien to the Self.

156. Maharshi:
One does not know the Self
owing to the interference of thoughts.
The Self is realized when thoughts subside.

157. Maharshi:
Concentration is not thinking one thing.
It is, on the other hand,
putting off all other thoughts
which obstruct the vision of our true nature.
All our efforts are only directed to
lifting the veil of ignorance.
Now it appears difficult to quell the thoughts.
In the regenerate state
it will be found more difficult to call in thoughts.
For are there things to think of?
There is only the Self.
Thoughts can function if there are objects.
But there are no objects.
How can thoughts arise at all?
The habit makes us believe
that it is difficult to cease thinking.
If the error is found out,
one would not be fool enough
to exert oneself unnecessarily by way of thinking.

158. Maharshi:
Be free from thoughts.
Do not hold on to anything.
They do not hold you.
Be yourself.

159. Maharshi:
Peace is always present.
Get rid of the disturbances to Peace.
This Peace is the Self.
The thoughts are the disturbances.
When free from them,
you are infinite intelligence, i.e., the Self.
There is Perfection and Peace.

160. Maharshi:
Only think of the root of the thoughts;
seek it and find it.
The Self shines by itself.
When that is found
the thoughts cease of their own accord.
That is freedom from bondage.

161. Maharshi:
If you are free from thoughts and yet aware,
you are that Perfect Being.

162. Maharshi:
When thoughts arise duality is present;
know it to be the ego,
and seek its source.
The degree of the absence of thoughts
is the measure of your progress
towards Self-Realization.
But Self-Realization itself
does not admit of progress;
it is ever the same.

163. Maharshi:
Thoughts must be checked
by seeking to whom they arise.
So you go to their Source,
where they do not arise.

Questioner:
Doubts are always arising.

Maharshi:
A doubt arises and is cleared;
another arises and that is cleared,
making way for another,
and so it goes on.
So there is no possibility
of clearing away all doubts.
See to whom the doubts arise.
Go to their Source and abide in it.
Then they cease to arise.
That is how doubts are to be cleared.

CHAPTER NINETEEN

LOOK WITHIN
(164 – 173)

164. Maharshi:
Because your outlook has been outward bent,
it has lost sight of the Self
and your vision is external.
The Self is not found in external objects.
Turn your look within and plunge down;
you will be the Self.

165. Questioner:
There are widespread disasters
spreading havoc in the world
e.g., famine and pestilence.
What is the cause of this state of affairs?

Maharshi:
To whom does all this appear?

Questioner:
That won't do.
I see misery around.

Maharshi:
You were not aware of the world and its sufferings
in your (deep dreamless) sleep;
you are conscious of them in your wakeful state.
Continue in that state
in which you were not afflicted by these.

That is to say,
when you are not aware of the world,
its sufferings do not affect you.
When you remain as the Self,
as in (deep dreamless) sleep,
the world and its sufferings will not affect you.
Therefore look within.
See the Self!
There will be an end of the world and its miseries.

166. Questioner:
What is to be done by us
for ameliorating the condition of the world?

Maharshi:
If you remain free from pain,
there will be no pain anywhere.
The trouble now is due to
your seeing the world externally
and also thinking that there is pain there.
Both the world and the pain are within you.
If you look within there will be no pain.

167. Questioner:
So it amounts to this –
that I should always look within.

Maharshi: Yes.

168. Maharshi:
Direct your look within and make it absolute.

169. Maharshi:
Because your outlook is externally directed
you speak of a *without*.
In that state you are advised to look *within*.

170. Maharshi:
Why waste time in such polemics?
Only turn your mind inward
and spend the time usefully.

171. Maharshi:
As the mind tends to go out
turn it inwards then and there.
It goes out owing to the habit
of looking for happiness outside oneself;
but the knowledge that the external objects
are not the cause of happiness
will keep it in check.

172. Maharshi:
You know that you are.
You cannot deny your existence
at any moment of time.
For you must be there in order to deny it.
This is understood by stilling your mind.
The mind is the outgoing faculty of the individual.
If that is turned within,
it becomes still in the course of time
and that "I-AM" alone prevails.
"I-AM" is the whole Truth.

173. Maharshi:
To turn the mind inward
the man must directly settle down in the 'I'.
Then there is an end of external activities
and perfect Peace prevails.

CHAPTER TWENTY

DESIRE, EAGERNESS AND DETERMINATION
(174 – 176)

174. Maharshi:
Subhechcha (the desire for enlightenment)
is the doorway for realization.

175. Maharshi:
Now, what should one do
to overcome the present ignorance.
Be eager to have the true knowledge.
As this eagerness grows
the wrong knowledge diminishes in strength
until it finally disappears.

176. Questioner:
When an endeavor is made to lead the right life
and to concentrate on the Self,
there is often downfall and break.
What is to be done?

    Maharshi:
It will come all right in the end.
There is the steady impulse of your determination
that sets you on your feet again
after every downfall and breakdown.
Gradually the obstacles are all overcome
and your current becomes stronger.
Everything comes right in the end.
Steady determination is what is required.

CHAPTER TWENTY ONE

WHO
(177 – 179)

177. Maharshi:
How do you meditate?

Questioner:
I begin to ask myself "Who am I?",
eliminate the body as not 'I',
the breath as not 'I',
the mind as not 'I'
and I am not able to proceed further.

Maharshi:
Well, that is so far as the intellect goes.
Your process is only intellectual.
Indeed, all the scriptures mention the process
only to guide the seeker to know the Truth.
The Truth cannot be directly pointed out.
Hence this intellectual process.
You see, the one who eliminates all the not I
cannot eliminate the 'I'.
This 'I' is only the ego or the 'I-thought'.
After the rising up of this 'I-thought',
all other thoughts arise.
The 'I-thought' is therefore the root-thought.
If the root is pulled out
all others are at the same time uprooted.

Therefore seek the root 'I',
question yourself "Who am I?";
find out its source.
Then all these will vanish
and the pure Self will remain ever.

178. Maharshi:
The one unalterable reality is Being.
Until you realize that state of pure being
you should pursue the inquiry.
If once you are established in it
there will be no further worry.
No one will inquire into the source of thoughts
unless thoughts arise.
So long as you think "I am walking,"
"I am writing,"
inquire who does it.

179. Maharshi:
Who are you now?
What is it that is born?
The Self is eternal and cannot be born.
The body appears and disappears
and your identity with it
makes you speak of birth and death.
See if the true significance of 'I' can ever take birth.
For whom is transmigration?

*Please use the contact form at seeseer.com
to let us know if reading
How to Practice Self Inquiry
was a good experience for you.*

*Five other books can be recommended
for those who wish to practice the Direct Path:*

*1. The Seven Steps to Awakening
is a collection of quotes by these Seven Sages:
Ramana Maharshi, Nisargadatta Maharaj,
Sankara, Vasistha, Muruganar, Sadhu Om
and Annamalai Swami.*

2. The Direct Means to Eternal Bliss.

*3. Contemplating Who am I?
by Bassui Tokusho, Yasutani Roshi
and Ramana Maharshi.*

*4. Self Abidance, abridged edition
by Srimati Margaret Coble.*

5. Powerful Quotes from Sankara.

*For information about those
and other spiritual books go to:*

www.seeseer.com

Made in the USA
Lexington, KY
28 September 2017